The **Rivers** of
the **Mandala**

The **Rivers** of the **Mandala**

Journey into the heart of Buddhism

Thames & Hudson

Simon Allix & Benoit de Vilmorin

Contents >

中华人民共和国
外国人旅行证
The People's Republic of China
Aliens' Travel Permit

->23 : Total Prostration

24 : Lake Manasarovar

38->39 : Geological Formation

60->61 : Sacred Cow / Am Staff

110->111 : Epilogue

34->35 : Trugo Monastery

88->89 : The Dolma Pass

90->91 : Guri Kund

36->37 : Padmasambhava

86->87 : Vajrayogini Cemetery

106->107 : Lhasa

25->27 : The Guge Kingdom

74->77 : North Face

98->99 : The Descent

30->31 : Wind-Horses

32->33 : Prayer Wheels

72->73 : Gems

52->53 : Gangri Chorten

50 : Darpoche

54->57 : Nyanri Monastery

44->45 : Coqen

84->85 : Ghazni, Afghanistan

46->49 : Lung-Tas

104->105 : Milarepa

to Thomas Allix
1971–2001

Design:
Simon Allix

Texts:
Benoit de Vilmorin
Jean-Pierre Allix *(page 38)*

Translation from French:
Marushka Vidovic

First published in 2004 in paperback
in the United States of America by
Thames & Hudson Inc., 500 Fifth Avenue,
New York, New York 10110

thamesandhudsonusa.com

Library of Congress
Catalog Card Number 2004100247
ISBN 0-500-28495-4

Printed in China

Introduction ›

There are destinations whose names, when spoken,
resonate in the heads of travellers like the echo of
cathedral prayers. A universal song calling mankind
to its very source, like that of the sirens who so
fascinated the mariners of old that they remained
haunted to the end of their days. A song full of
mysticism, dedicated to the elevation of the soul,
in which the purity of the voices streams up towards
the mountain tops, every note a victory in the quest
for self-awareness.

Barren heights, rocky valleys, glacial winds and a
sensation of having arrived at the end of the world:
Mount Kailash is a far cry from a reassuring Eden
that might comfort our simple mortal souls. And yet
the Tibetans compare it to the mandala that depicts
their beliefs. The mandala, a complex design made
out of pigments by monks, is a tool for meditation
and also for initiation. It is a circle built out of a
number of coloured layers, whose curved harmony
is broken by quadrilateral shapes as if to remind
us of the complexity of the natural and spiritual
elements that make up our being. When wandering
Kailash's foothills, we are beings no bigger than
ants, crossing a rough, desert-like land, but just
as the rivers and their tributaries are fed by their
sources, we are enriched by our awareness of the
essential nature of things.

Thomas & Simon ›

The heroes of this story are two brothers, Thomas and Simon. Born into a family of artists, with a thirst for adventure and knowledge, they see curiosity as the greatest of qualities, the only thing that keeps the flame of enthusiasm alive. Following the primeval instinct to discover the world, and the inner and mysterious quest of our existence, they trod the paths of Pakistan, wandered the Tibetan valleys and mingled with the hordes of India.

And if each journey is one step won over our mortal destiny, it also allows us to enrich ourselves with other cultures that may then turn our lives around. This was the case with Thomas, who as the years went by became a true 'Kailashophile' and a scholar of Buddhist thought. No less than three journeys around the sacred mountain made him wise, well aware that even a vagabond may be noble if he fights ignorance, and that the thirst for liberty can be seen in the reflection of our inner peace.

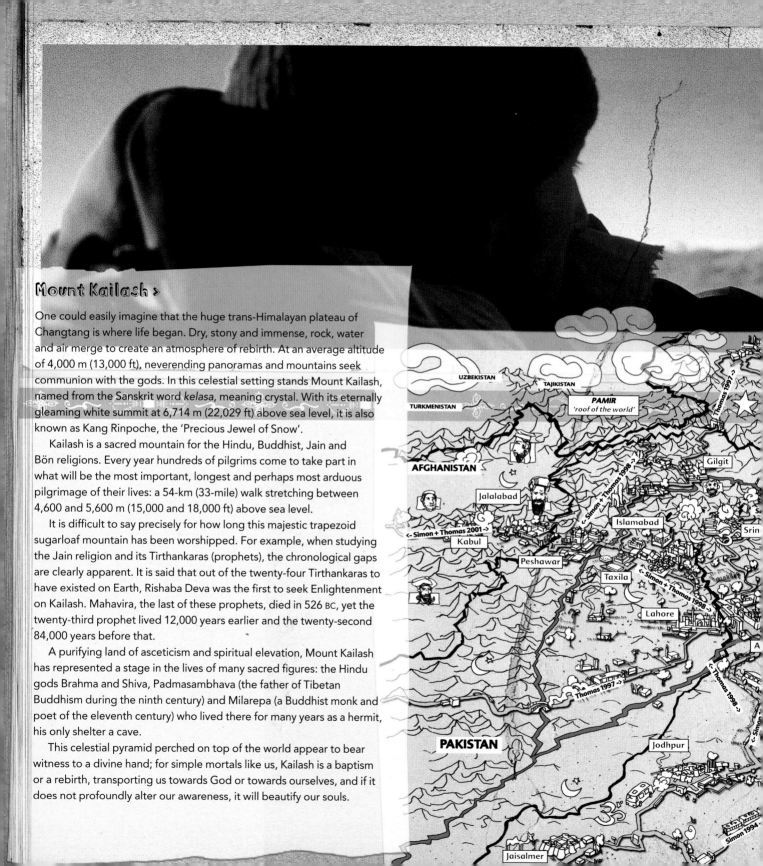

Mount Kailash >

One could easily imagine that the huge trans-Himalayan plateau of Changtang is where life began. Dry, stony and immense, rock, water and air merge to create an atmosphere of rebirth. At an average altitude of 4,000 m (13,000 ft), neverending panoramas and mountains seek communion with the gods. In this celestial setting stands Mount Kailash, named from the Sanskrit word *kelasa*, meaning crystal. With its eternally gleaming white summit at 6,714 m (22,029 ft) above sea level, it is also known as Kang Rinpoche, the 'Precious Jewel of Snow'.

Kailash is a sacred mountain for the Hindu, Buddhist, Jain and Bön religions. Every year hundreds of pilgrims come to take part in what will be the most important, longest and perhaps most arduous pilgrimage of their lives: a 54-km (33-mile) walk stretching between 4,600 and 5,600 m (15,000 and 18,000 ft) above sea level.

It is difficult to say precisely for how long this majestic trapezoid sugarloaf mountain has been worshipped. For example, when studying the Jain religion and its Tirthankaras (prophets), the chronological gaps are clearly apparent. It is said that out of the twenty-four Tirthankaras to have existed on Earth, Rishaba Deva was the first to seek Enlightenment on Kailash. Mahavira, the last of these prophets, died in 526 BC, yet the twenty-third prophet lived 12,000 years earlier and the twenty-second 84,000 years before that.

A purifying land of asceticism and spiritual elevation, Mount Kailash has represented a stage in the lives of many sacred figures: the Hindu gods Brahma and Shiva, Padmasambhava (the father of Tibetan Buddhism during the ninth century) and Milarepa (a Buddhist monk and poet of the eleventh century) who lived there for many years as a hermit, his only shelter a cave.

This celestial pyramid perched on top of the world appear to bear witness to a divine hand; for simple mortals like us, Kailash is a baptism or a rebirth, transporting us towards God or towards ourselves, and if it does not profoundly alter our awareness, it will beautify our souls.

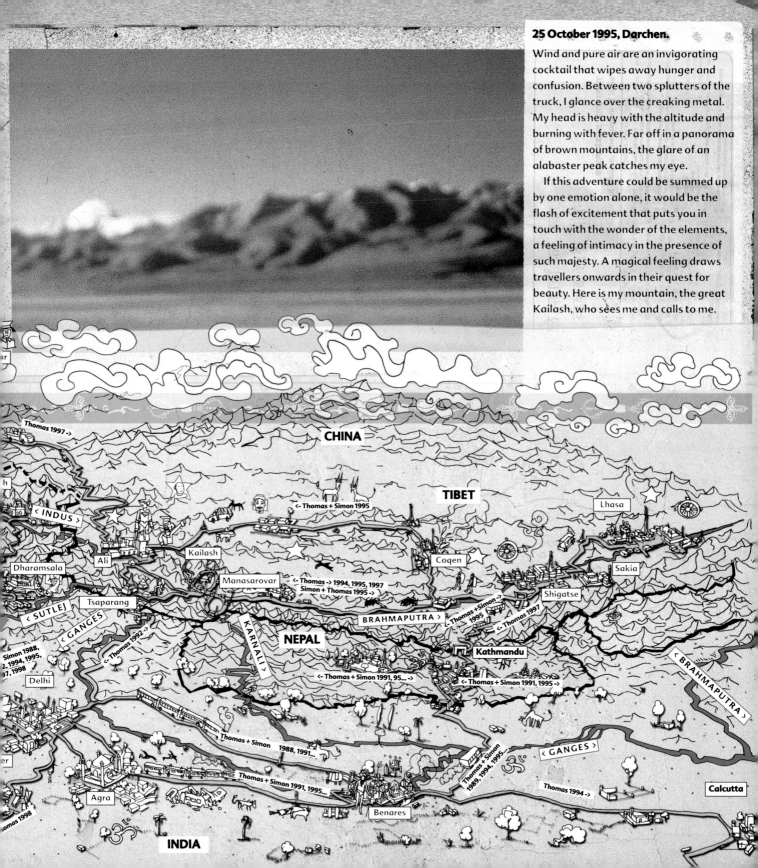

25 October 1995, Darchen.

Wind and pure air are an invigorating cocktail that wipes away hunger and confusion. Between two splutters of the truck, I glance over the creaking metal. My head is heavy with the altitude and burning with fever. Far off in a panorama of brown mountains, the glare of an alabaster peak catches my eye.

If this adventure could be summed up by one emotion alone, it would be the flash of excitement that puts you in touch with the wonder of the elements, a feeling of intimacy in the presence of such majesty. A magical feeling draws travellers onwards in their quest for beauty. Here is my mountain, the great Kailash, who sees me and calls to me.

Holy Mountain ›

As far back as it is possible to go in the history of civilization, mankind has always had a special reverence for high places. Be they symbols of strength or divine power, mountains elevate common mortals towards the sky, towards wisdom and achievement. On their journey to Mount Kailash, pilgrims walk around the mountain, emulating the sun's journey around the earth – the circle being one of creation's most perfect figures, and for Buddhists the symbol of the wheel of existence, the continuing cycle of death and rebirth.

Humans see the circle as a path to self-discovery. From ritual tribal dances

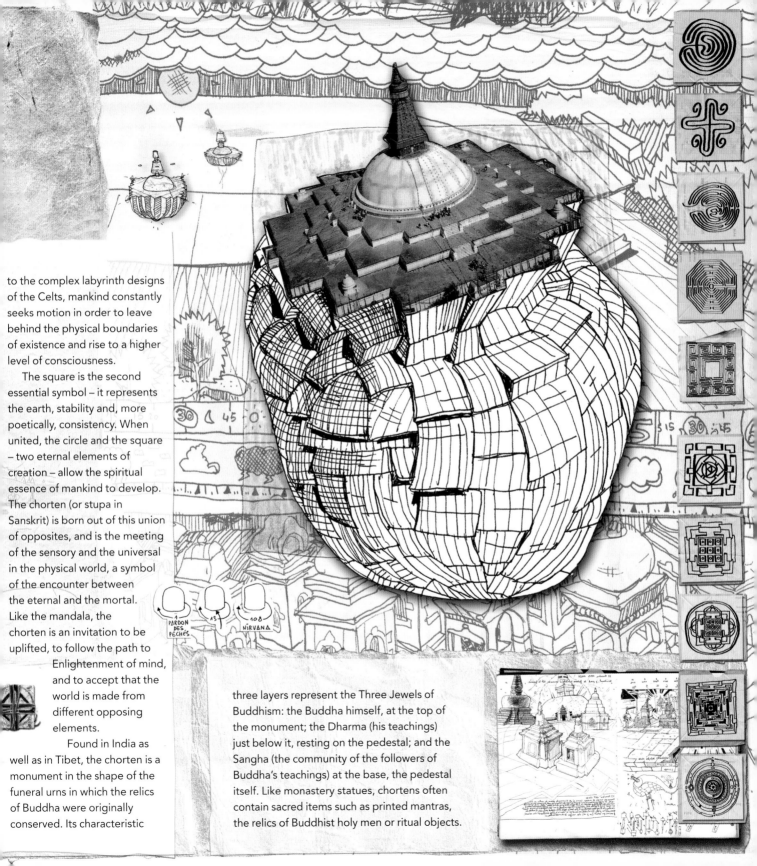

to the complex labyrinth designs of the Celts, mankind constantly seeks motion in order to leave behind the physical boundaries of existence and rise to a higher level of consciousness.

The square is the second essential symbol – it represents the earth, stability and, more poetically, consistency. When united, the circle and the square – two eternal elements of creation – allow the spiritual essence of mankind to develop. The chorten (or stupa in Sanskrit) is born out of this union of opposites, and is the meeting of the sensory and the universal in the physical world, a symbol of the encounter between the eternal and the mortal. Like the mandala, the chorten is an invitation to be uplifted, to follow the path to Enlightenment of mind, and to accept that the world is made from different opposing elements.

Found in India as well as in Tibet, the chorten is a monument in the shape of the funeral urns in which the relics of Buddha were originally conserved. Its characteristic

PARDON DES PÉCHÉS

13

108 NIRVANA

three layers represent the Three Jewels of Buddhism: the Buddha himself, at the top of the monument; the Dharma (his teachings) just below it, resting on the pedestal; and the Sangha (the community of the followers of Buddha's teachings) at the base, the pedestal itself. Like monastery statues, chortens often contain sacred items such as printed mantras, the relics of Buddhist holy men or ritual objects.

Transport ›

Getting around in Tibet is not an easy task, particularly without a four-wheel drive. Resourcefulness is usually the key. In the West, backpackers have well-kept facilities and cheap public transport at their disposal. There are a few buses that will get you around the outskirts of Lhasa, but as soon as you need to travel hundreds of kilometres, the only way is to hitchhike, paying your way. The rare vehicles that agree to take you are often goods trucks. Offering a ride in less than comfortable conditions (in the back, wedged between two petrol cans, a goat and a few local passengers) they relieve you of the tidy sum of one *yuan* per kilometre (0,15 €). There are several advantages in taking this type of transport. Firstly the thrill factor, as it is not unusual to be thrown around due to a badly negotiated bump. Secondly, it provides the traveller not only with breathtaking scenery but also a good kilo of dust per day!

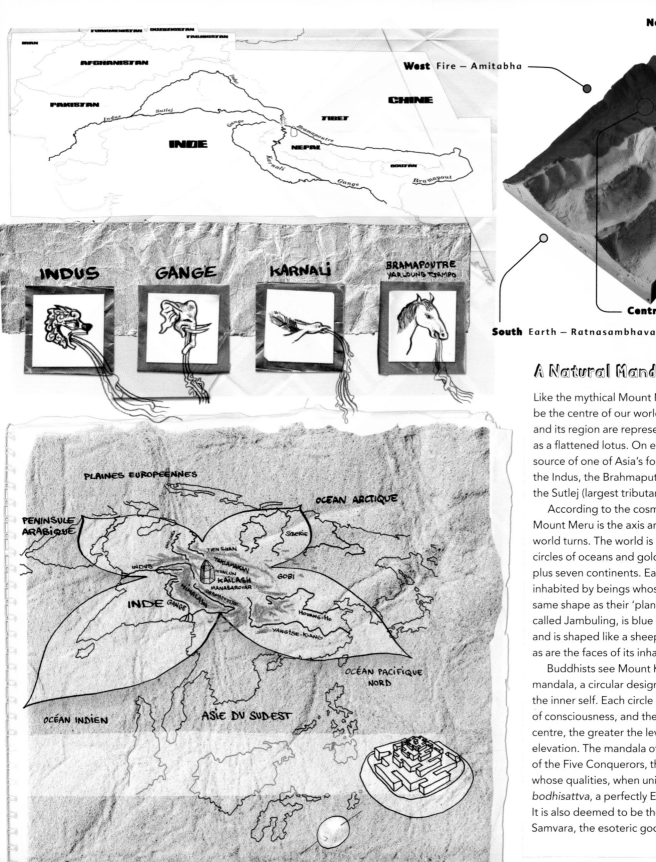

INDUS   GANGE   KARNALI   BRAMAPOUTRE YARLOUNG TSAMPO

A Natural Mandala >

Like the mythical Mount Meru, thought to be the centre of our world, Mount Kailash and its region are represented by Buddhists as a flattened lotus. On each petal lies the source of one of Asia's four greatest rivers: the Indus, the Brahmaputra, the Karnali and the Sutlej (largest tributary of the Ganges).

According to the cosmogony of the Jain, Mount Meru is the axis around which the world turns. The world is made up of seven circles of oceans and golden mountains, plus seven continents. Each continent is inhabited by beings whose faces are the same shape as their 'planet'. Our world, called Jambuling, is blue (so far so good!) and is shaped like a sheep's shoulder blade, as are the faces of its inhabitants….

Buddhists see Mount Kailash as a huge mandala, a circular design that symbolizes the inner self. Each circle represents a level of consciousness, and the closer it is to the centre, the greater the level of spiritual elevation. The mandala of Kailash is that of the Five Conquerors, the five Buddhas whose qualities, when united, produce a *bodhisattva*, a perfectly Enlightened being. It is also deemed to be the throne of Samvara, the esoteric god that symbolizes

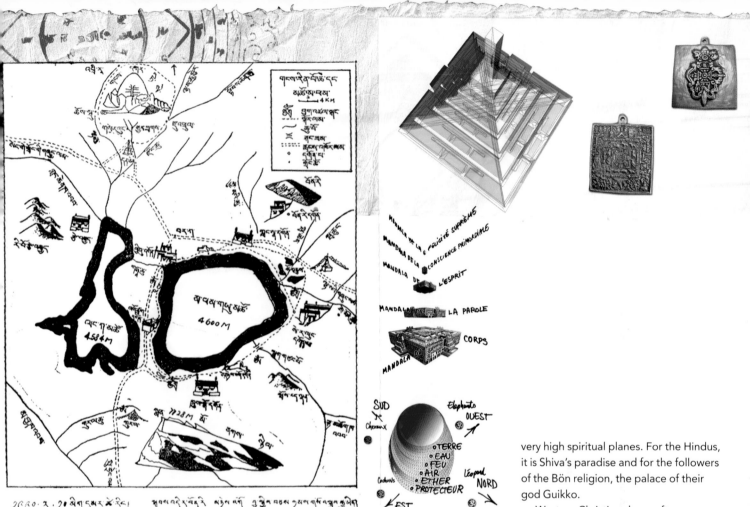

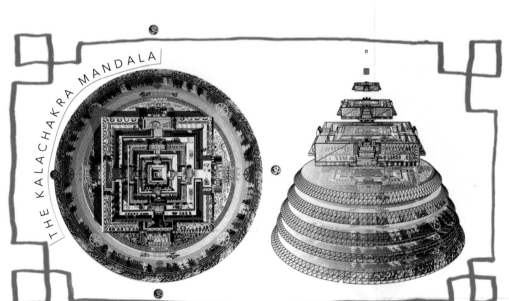

THE KALACHAKRA MANDALA

1990 · 2 · 10 MIGMAR TSERING

very high spiritual planes. For the Hindus, it is Shiva's paradise and for the followers of the Bön religion, the palace of their god Guikko.

Western Christians have often compared the mandala to the labyrinths that can be found in many French cathedrals; these may be circular (Bayeux, Poitiers or Sens) or octagonal (Chartres, Amiens). The symbol was adopted from the early Celts and made popular by the legend of Theseus and the Minotaur; reaching the centre represents the power of grace triumphing over the forces of evil.

The pagan reading of the labyrinth follows the medieval concept of the meaning of life: moving forward, dealing with snares, retracing one's steps and hopefully finding the way. In both forms of labyrinth, imaginary or constructed, the same notion of progression may be found: man seeks out his own truth and vanquishes his demons.

1 November 1995. From Darchen to Huore.

Darchen, 5 a.m. — The billiard tables no longer echo with the nervous laughter of enthusiastic players. The cold clings to us as we take our first morning steps. Hunched over, our muscles tense, our bodies and clothes merge into one. Our outer layers slowly develop an icy crust and we end up waiting for the truck almost frozen. Thomas has managed to negotiate two seats from pilgrims on their way back to Lhasa who have agreed to drop us off in Huore.

The dawn temperature in November plummets to as low as -20 °C. The noise of the approaching truck breaks the magical silence of the deserted early morning, a few blessed

moments in which man seems to belong to nature, a witness to its awakening.

We climb in the back and begin our journey. Just a few metres further on, I realize that the next few hours will be torture. Thomas and I can no longer feel anything, not our clothes, nor our limbs or bodies, absolutely nothing. The cold has well and truly anaesthetized us.

The other pilgrims stop us from sleeping by shaking us as soon as we begin to drop off. It will take our vehicle an eternity to go the short distance from Darchen to Huore. The trip is one of constant suffering. At one point, the truck tries to cross a river and gets stuck. I grab the chance to relieve myself, but in the intense cold, I find it impossible to use my hands. With my trousers down, I spray my fingers with urine. The effort required to do all of this hypnotizes me.

It is in this state of stupor that we arrive in Huore. Our bodies are stiff and no one in the truck even says a word to wish us luck. For the beginning of our pilgrimage, we are truly penitent. A few days later, we learn that a group of Japanese people died during a similar journey — frozen to death while travelling through a pass.

A man notices that we look like survivors and invites us to follow him. Thomas pulls a contented face; we must look truly wretched as our rescuer seems alarmed! We sit down around the stove. He takes my hands and puts them over the embers. The dried dung used as fuel is just a few centimetres away from me; the Tibetans prefer to keep the rare commodity of wood for nobler tasks, such as building temples or houses. Amazingly, I can't feel a thing. Time seems to come to a standstill. Dumbfounded, I watch one of the children sipping *raki* (an alcoholic drink) while Thomas drinks his tea. The hot drink made of butter and *tsampa* (grilled barley flour) slowly begins to revive us; my hands start to unstiffen and get back their feeling. After two hours that feel like fifteen, we finally set off again to travel the last ten kilometres to Lake Manasarovar. The ground is crinkled like wet cardboard that has dried in the sun, making our hike even harder. After hours of walking, we finally see Manasarovar, with its turquoise water and the first pilgrims prostrating themselves on the ground.

With a small gesture of complicity, Thomas lets me know that his heart is beating a little faster.

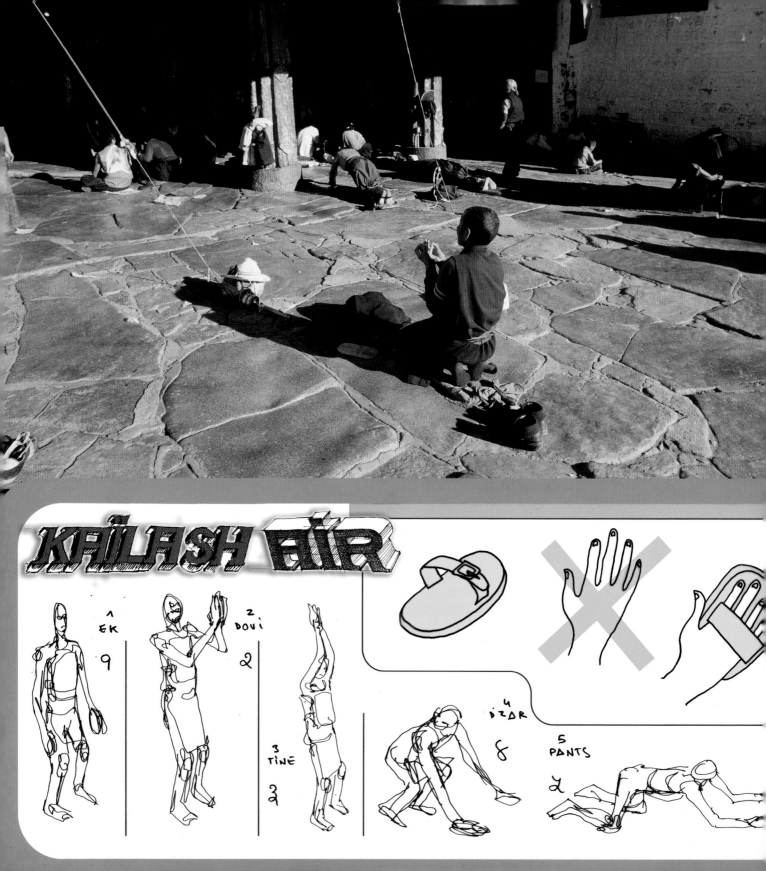

KAILASH AIR

1. EK
9

2. DOVI
2

3. TINE
3

4. IZDR
8

5. PANTS
2

Total Prostration >

For anyone unaccustomed to religious ceremonies in which suffering is synonymous with purification and forgiveness, total prostration is one of the most impressive of rituals.

Tibetan Buddhists, both men and women, hang planks of wood or protective leather flaps onto their clothes to prevent them from hurting themselves too much and also to make it easier to slide along the dry and rocky ground. Moving in small groups, the pilgrims lie down flat on the ground and then get up, repeating this gesture of abnegation over and over again, leaving the marks of their effort behind them. In this way, pilgrims become physically as well as spiritually absorbed by their quest, forging a connection with the sacred elements at the most basic level.

The sight of these pilgrims reminds me of some of the Catholic practices that can be seen in Europe. On the island of Tinos, Greek pilgrims, almost as soon as they arrive, get face down on the ground or on all fours; they then crawl or even

roll on their sides all the way to the chapel where the blessing of the Virgin awaits them. At Croach Patrick and on Station Island, Irish pilgrims stay awake all night long and then climb the mountains barefoot or even sometimes on their knees. At Mount Kailash, the pilgrimage in total prostration takes three weeks.

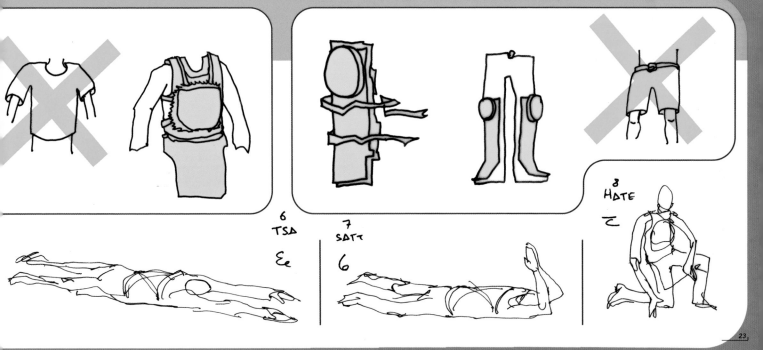

2 November 1995. Lake Manasarovar.

The altitude, to which I thought I had become accustomed, seems to give me panic attacks, or maybe it's down to the shortage of food or its complete lack of variety. I try to empty my mind and forget the packets of freeze-dried pasta that invariably make up the mainstay of my meals. While Thomas performs his ablutions in the icy waters of the Manasarovar, I implore the great and pure forces that forged these landscapes to deliver me. There is no sweeter nourishment than this air hitting me in waves. I breathe in deeply and all of a sudden, my mind is filled with images of

roast chickens, rare steaks, marinated fish, juicy fruit; a veritable feast projected like a movie in front of my eyes. I am swimming in a cartoon; I am the big bad wolf dreaming of whole legs of ham, and juicy doggie bones, dribbling with excitement. I open my eyes. What a shame... nothing has changed!

Thomas has joined me and, winking, holds out a little mahogany-coloured stone. Maybe it's one of those famous medicinal stones used by Tibetan monks or by Native Americans to take the edge off their hunger?

The Guge Kingdom ❯

To the north-west of Kailash, the ruins of Tsaparang and Tholing rise up from the middle of enormous canyons and steep-sided valleys, whose sides are garlanded with the scars of erosion.

Crumbling temples, damaged statues: the passing centuries, invaders and revolutions have left little of the ancient Guge Kingdom, founded in the tenth century while the country was reeling from the ❯

political chaos that followed the assassination of King Tri Ralpachen. His brother Langdarma took the throne and reinstated the Bön religion, while the Buddhists were persecuted and forced to flee. Nevertheless, the monk Lhalung Pelgyi Dorje succeeded in killing the cruel sovereign during a theatre performance.

Tibet was then split into numerous strongholds governed by its former aristocracy. One of Langdarma's sons, Osung, created a small state in the west of the country: the Guge Kingdom. Osung was succeeded by Yeshe Ö, a key figure in the second dissemination of Tibetan Buddhism. He sent twenty-one monks to India to translate the sacred texts. These included Rinchen Zangpo, who would become the greatest translator of Sanskrit works and who remained there for seventeen years, sending back many Indian scholars who founded over a hundred monasteries throughout the region. A Turkish army captured King Yeshe Ö and held his family to ransom, but the king's wish was to perpetuate his kingdom's religious standing and he sacrificed himself, ordering that the money be spent on bringing the renowned Indian master Atisha to his realm. After Atisha had spent three years at Tholing Monastery, where he wrote his celebrated work *Lamp For the Path to Enlightenment*, Rinchen Zangpo, then eighty-five years old, encouraged him to spend the rest of his life in the mountains in meditation. This he did, often on Mount Kailash, until his death.

Tsatsas ›

On the outskirts of Tsaparang, at the bottom of holes in the rock, dozens of *tsatsas* left by pilgrims can often be found. These little statues bearing the effigies of deities, or in the shape of chortens, are made out of a mixture of earth and funeral ashes. A printed mantra is placed inside them. The relatives of the deceased leave them in sacred places along their way, in memory of the dead.

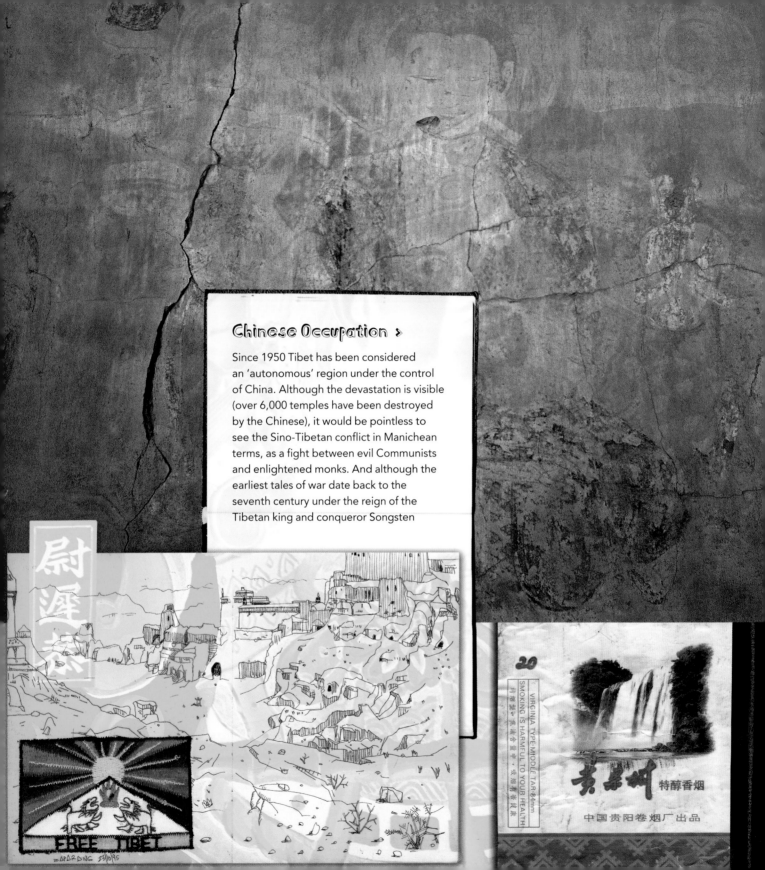

Chinese Occupation ›

Since 1950 Tibet has been considered an 'autonomous' region under the control of China. Although the devastation is visible (over 6,000 temples have been destroyed by the Chinese), it would be pointless to see the Sino-Tibetan conflict in Manichean terms, as a fight between evil Communists and enlightened monks. And although the earliest tales of war date back to the seventh century under the reign of the Tibetan king and conqueror Songsten

FREE TIBET

Gampo, it has never been clear 'who started it', as they say in school.

As stressed by Giuseppe Tucci in his book *Tibet: Land of Snows*, it is wiser to think the two countries as 'two entirely different conceptions face to face: an inflexible abstract scheme, all figures and duties, on the one hand, and on the other a fundamental anarchy of invisible presences that control us but which we can dominate, if we know their secret. Facts on the one side; imagination on the other. The life of man confined within time and space, in the service of a community which seeks economic and social betterment at the cost of individual freedom, with the new ideology; affirmation of the personality through its dialogue with the transcendent world of the divine, belittling of the real in comparison with the invisible, transcendence overriding time and space, with the Tibetan spiritual tradition.'

Wind-Horses ›

In Tibet the bond between nature and religion is omnipresent. From the magnificence of its landscapes to the harshness of everyday life, the strength of the elements is such that it is echoed in religion. Is this because, prior to the Chinese invasion, 20 per cent of the population had taken holy orders and the temples were the country's main cultural centres, or is it perhaps the legacy of the ancient animistic Bön faith and its belief in the forces of nature?

The answer may be found in the religious practices that pay homage to deities and their habitats. These include *lung-ta*s or 'wind-horses', which may take the form of flags or small printed pieces of paper that are thrown into the wind, the only element able to communicate with all the others. Decorated with the image of a horse, Tibet's protector, these offerings bring blessings to the environment and embody the Buddhist wish to deliver all beings from suffering.

ༀ་མ་ཎི་པ་དྨེ་ཧཱུྃ

Prayer Wheels >

Everything in Tibet has a spiritual
dimension, from the people's
respect for nature to their quest for
Enlightenment. Every moment not spent on domestic
chores can be used to deepen one's quest or increase one's
merit. One of the methods that Tibetans use to do this is
the prayer wheel. This is a metal cylinder that contains
printed mantras and may be set on a base (inside a temple
or a monastery) or a handle. It is turned while the traditional
chant *Om Mani Padme Hum* is recited.

   During their circumambulation of Mount Kailash,
pilgrims turn the wheel of Dharma, their own inner spirit
that uses the Buddha's teachings to increase their
awareness and enhance their initiation.

3 November 1995. Lake Manasarovar.

The golden red glints in the earth remind me of the story
of the Great Nugget that Thomas told me last night.
In the early twentieth century, Tibetans digging a hole in
the rock found a gold nugget the size of a dog. Enthralled
with its beauty but alarmed by its incredible size, they
decided to give it to the Dalai Lama, because Buddhists
are unconcerned about material riches and they feared
the desires that such a treasure might awaken. To prevent
it from falling prey to looters and treasure hunters, the
Dalai Lama recommended that the nugget be returned
to its natural element and suggested placing it in the
middle of Lake Manasarovar.

3 November 1995. Trugo Monastery.

We have left the banks of the lake and headed for Trugo Monastery, where once the monk Atisha stayed. Its name means 'door to the baths' because of the traditional ablutions carried out by the pilgrims at Lake Manasarovar. A two-kilometre path takes us to the monastery gate, which does justice to the magnificent panorama that lies before us. We are penniless, and the monks offer us a place to stay that is dusty and freezing cold.

The view consoles us and we lose ourselves in contemplating the horizon, in the hope of spotting the Tree of Knowledge, which, according to the legend, sits in the middle of Lake Manasarovar. This symbolic tree, beneath whose shade Buddha sat in meditation after six years of asceticism, represents both celestial knowledge and sensory awareness of the environment for many faiths, along with protection and nourishment. The tree bears fruit that may only be seen by the Enlightened and that provide food for its protectors, the nagas — dragons of wisdom that live at the bottom of Lake Manasarovar. Inhabited by Parvati, the consort of Shiva who resides on Mount Kailash, Lake Manasarovar is linked with the faculty of reason (*manas*) by Hindus. A bodhisattva sits on each of the lotus flowers that cover its surface. This allegory encourages disciples to feed on the fruits of knowledge in order to raise their consciousness from the depths of the mind to the surface where the petals catch the sun's light, depicting the state of Enlightenment and showing their wish to turn upwards, towards Mount Kailash and its summit.

Padmasambhava ›

The Tibetans' worship of Padmasambhava ('the lotus-born') is such that they see him as the second Buddha, the reincarnation of the Buddha Amitabha and a manifestation of the historical Buddha Sakyamuni. He is a complex figure who is said to have lived for several thousands of years and whose many existences are made up of multiple interpretations in which chronological reality and symbolic meaning are merged. Despite this multiplicity, Padmasambhava is an actual historical figure. He was an Indian sage called upon by the Buddhist Tibetan King Trisong Detsen in the eighth century to assist in the construction of the Samye Monastery and to spread Buddha's teachings to the Land of Snows. He was behind the Sanskrit-Tibetan translation of the Buddhist canon and, once the monastery was finished, he brought monks there who spent fifty years translating the 103 volumes of the Buddha's teachings and other sacred texts.

Although he is not strictly speaking a divinity, the life of Padmasambhava (also known as Guru Rinpoche) has become merged with the legends surrounding it. Like that of Milarepa, his story is full of symbolic events, extraordinary abilities and also reprehensible acts.

He was born on the pure fresh waters of Lake Dhanakosha in the region of Oddiyana, situated along the present-day border of Pakistan and Afghanistan. The animals of this paradisal land came to greet the birth of the child, who was born looking like a boy of eight. Meanwhile, King Indrabodhi travelled to the Island of Jewels in search of riches, because he had used up his own wealth in acts of great generosity so as to benefit from divine mercy. On his return journey, the heirless king found this miraculous child seated on a lotus flower and adopted him, later giving him the hand of his daughter, Princess Bhasadhara.

But this comfortable lifestyle was not to Padmasambhava's liking. He committed crimes in order to flee from the kingdom and hid in a cemetery where he gave himself up to contemplation and yogic disciplines.

Ordained as a monk following a trip to Benares where he had been initiated, as well as receiving medical, linguistic and astrological training, he then headed for the Zahor Kingdom with a view to converting it. He found refuge in a religious community of women, one of whom was the beautiful Mandarava, the daughter of Zahor's sovereign, but the king sent his troops to take the young monk captive. Padmasambhava was judged and sentenced to be burnt at the stake. However, the king soon learned that the fire had been burning continuously for seven days, and intrigued, he went to see for himself. His surprise was even greater when he discovered that the pyre had transformed into a huge lake on which Padmasambhava could be seen, sitting on a lotus flower.

The **south**-facing slope looks towards India, its monsoons and its teeming millions. 500 km (300 miles) to the Ganges at Allahabad with Benares another 100 km (60 miles) further on. 1,500 km (900 miles) and we reach the Indian Ocean.

From the **west**-facing slope, Lahore in Pakistan is 650 km (400 miles) away; Kandahar in Afghanistan, 1,500 km (900 miles); Basra in Iraq, 3,000 km (1,800 miles) away; Jerusalem, 4,500 km (2,800 miles) and Agadir in Morocco 8,500 km (5,300 miles).

Mount Kailash
Altitude: 6,714 m (22,029 ft)
Position: 31° 03' N, 81° 20' E

Geological Formation ›

The Himalayas are said to be 'young' mountains, but it should not be forgotten that their upheaval (resulting from the collision between the Indian and South Asian tectonic plates) began thirty-five million years ago. The plates continue to move some 5 cm (2 inches) per annum, so the process is continuing before our eyes. Erosion (unlike elsewhere on the planet) does not occur after the upheaval; it accompanies it. It could be said that the mountain is demolished by the erosion, but at the same time, it is being created by the

forces of upheaval. The Himalayan range, with its width, relief and height, is therefore the result of an unstable balance between opposing forces that has been taking place for thirty-five million years – the rhythm an irregular one, sometimes accelerating, sometimes slowing down.

Rock torn down by erosion from the mountain ranges accumulates in front of the mountain in immensely thick layers, one on top of the other, like the pages of a book. If the folding phase speeds up,

this matter is caught up in the turmoil. The huge mass of debris lying in front of the mountains folds and rises up. A strange quirk of fate occurs in which the stratified mass, the result of erosion, becomes itself prey to erosion. This is the geological history of the Kailash range.

As for the pyramid of Kailash itself, with its four characteristic sides, it owes the privilege of rising above its surroundings to its central location. This almost geometrical summit is nothing more than the last stronghold of

The **north** face. Yinning, on the border between Kazakhstan and China is 4,500 km (2,800 miles) away; the Arctic Ocean and its ice flows, 15,000 km (9,300 miles).

Travelling from the **east**, Lhasa is at a distance of 900 km (560 miles), Chengdu 2,200 km (1,400 miles) and Shanghai 3,900 km (2,400 miles). Much further still lies San Diego, California.

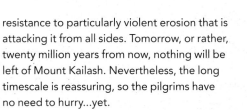

resistance to particularly violent erosion that is attacking it from all sides. Tomorrow, or rather, twenty million years from now, nothing will be left of Mount Kailash. Nevertheless, the long timescale is reassuring, so the pilgrims have no need to hurry...yet.

Darchen ›

For pilgrims, the village of Darchen is the last link with civilization before beginning the journey to Mount Kailash. This village has always welcomed men and women of all faiths, a sign of its innate tolerance. The name comes from *Dar-Chen*, which means 'the great standard' and refers to the huge pole decorated with prayer flags that marks the path to Darpoche, the sacred site situated a few hours walk from the village.

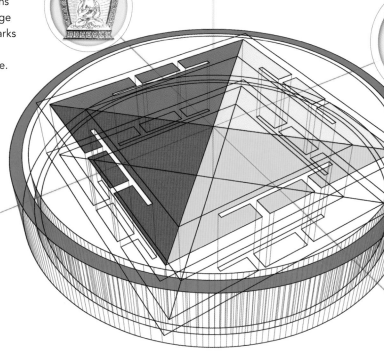

The Five Conquerors ›

The spiritual belief systems of Bön, Hinduism and Buddhism have all left their mark on the Kailash region, with sacred places and symbols dedicated to gods or deities. Although these figures do not have the same significance for every faith, they nonetheless play the same role as a basis for meditation for those undertaking this long journey. The pilgrims also feel the power of phenomena more strongly in an environment that a divine presence has shared. The very mention of these remarkable beings and their lives encourages the pilgrims on their way; and to advance towards the very place where they once lived is a source of inspiration.

A mandala symbolically depicting the pilgrimage to Kailash contains five poles, each of which is represented by an element and a divinity to which it is connected. These five divinities are known as the Dhyani Buddhas or Jina, meaning 'conquerors', and all Buddhas are descended from them (excluding the primordial Buddhas). They are depicted almost in the very centre of the mandala as all of their combined qualities are essential to attain Enlightenment and become a *bodhisattva*. Each of the Dhyani Buddhas reigns over a pure field, an equivalent to the Judeo–Christian heaven, where beings with the necessary attributes may escape from *samsara* (the cycle of existence).

Darchen (to the south) is the territory of Ratnasambhava ('born of a jewel'). The element connected with him is Earth and his colour is yellow. Ratnasambhava holds in his hands a divine wish-fulfilling jewel, the *chintamani*.

He also represents the nature of mind, the source of good. His right hand makes the *mudra* (sign) of giving. In the pure state of Enlightenment, he is the embodiment of the world of sensations. He banishes the poison of pride and transforms it into equality in order to reach a single pure essence: emptiness. Ratnasambhava's main activity is spiritual enrichment, illustrated by his yellow colour, which symbolizes gold and good fortune.

Nyanri (to the west) is dedicated to Amitabh ('infinite light'), whose element is Fire. Amitabh embodies discriminating wisdom, which enable

him to see all things as separate but equal. To make this wisdom possible, he frees minds from the poison of desire. He acts for the good of others, with no attachment. This altruistic and egalitarian approach allows Amitabha to draw other beings to him through the strength of his love. The colour red that is associated with him is an indication of this, and the lotus that he holds in his hand is a sign of purity.

Dolma (to the north) is inhabited by Amoghasiddhi ('almighty conqueror'), whose colour is green and who represents the sphere of Air. Within pure Enlightenment, Amoghasiddhi represents volition, all that results from willpower. These results may be positive (compassion, faith) or negative (contempt, desire). He embodies the wisdom of perfected action, a purification of consciousness that may include everyone, pure or not. With this wisdom and freedom from the poison of envy, one can merge with

all others, and the realization of wisdom can be achieved. This guiding role is depicted by Amoghasiddhi's gesture of protection, and justifies his violent nature, which is only used in order to eliminate obstacles that hinder the good of living beings.

The descent from Kailash (to the east) is ruled by Akshobhya ('the immovable one') and the element of Water. He holds a *vajra* or 'thunderbolt' sceptre in his left hand as a sign of pure consciousness, and his right hand is held in a *mudra* known as 'calling the earth to witness'. Akshobhya's colour is blue and he embodies mirrorlike wisdom, which reveals the true nature of things and combats the poison of hatred. His pure consciousness is like the pilgrim completing his long journey, finally free from effort and reaching his goal.

Mount Kailash itself is associated with Vairochana, which means 'the radiant one'; his colour is white and his element is Ether. He carries the wheel of Dharma. On the scale of

pure Enlightenment, he represents the ability to perceive forms and their constituent matter, the body. But it is as the expression of wisdom of *dharmadatu*, the realm of truth, that he may be truly likened to Mount Kailash. The mountain is eternal and shining, a majestic and gigantic pedestal that, like the *dharmadatu*, is the place of the essence of mind, provided that it is freed from the poison of ignorance. This is why Vairochana's gesture is the turning of the wheel of Dharma, symbolizing the Buddha's teachings.

中华人民共和国

外国人旅行证

The People's Republic of China

Aliens' Travel Permit

字 第 95 10 4 号

No.

15 October 1995, Ali and the Alien Travel Permit.

Ali, a hell built from cubes. Chinese Ali. Flash Ali. Looking like a science-fiction film set, nothing here in this pile of shiny huts is reassuring to a traveller who has just escaped the desert valleys. Quite appropriately, it is in this administrative centre that we have to buy our 'Alien Travel Permit'. After weeks spent being sent from one official bureau to another, we finally leave with our precious passport that will open the doors of Kailash to us. A line of satellite dishes leads us to the nearest shop where we celebrate our extraterrestrial status in style with a piece of soft lard. The next step is to find a means of transport, preferably not one of those tourist buses that the Tibetans say leave clouds of green banknotes in their wake.

SITUATION VILLES AU TIBET

Legend:

- Street
- Police station
- Shops and restaurants
- Temple
- Hospital
- Hotel
- Bank
- School
- Police security point
- Radar

BONUS

- Dog
- Goat
- Sheep
- Crow
- Bird
- Mouse or rat
- Yak
- Horse
- Various objects

MISCELLANEOUS

- Monk
- Chinese
- Tibetan
- Police
- Taxi
- Taxi
- Truck
- Bicycle
- Nomad

- Motorcycle
- Sidecar
- 4-wheel drive
- Sports ground
- House
- Market
- Roundabout

11 October 1995. Coqen.

Still waiting, for days on end, without anything happening, in a town where nothing ever happens. The show must go on, boredom must be fought just to survive, otherwise we'll end up drowning in a jug of Chang beer. We have to fight. Big brother, the grudges of the past must be dealt with, now or never: my toy that you broke, your playhouse that I destroyed, my watch that you burnt, saying it was for a scientific experiment.

We both play a game of 'The Good, The Bad and The Ugly'. The deserted street is perfect for a brotherly duel. The corner of Thomas's lip trembles, and he flashes a sadistic look in my direction and spits. I get up slowly, spreading my arms, ready to fend off a sudden attack. I grip a packet of freeze-dried noodles firmly in my hand, Thomas chooses a pair of wet shoes. The sun is just a few degrees away from the horizon. We improvise a song of whistles and tongue clicking, at the end of which — in accordance with tradition — we'll see which of us is quickest on the draw.

Our huge shadows add the final touch of Wild West authenticity. I crack a few noodles, to show him what I am capable of. Suddenly the look in Thomas's eyes changes from one of tension to one of surprise — he drops his stinking weapon and turns around. A Chinese restaurant owner crosses the street with a pot of steaming soup, its smell enticing. We simultaneously put our weapons away and hurry after him.

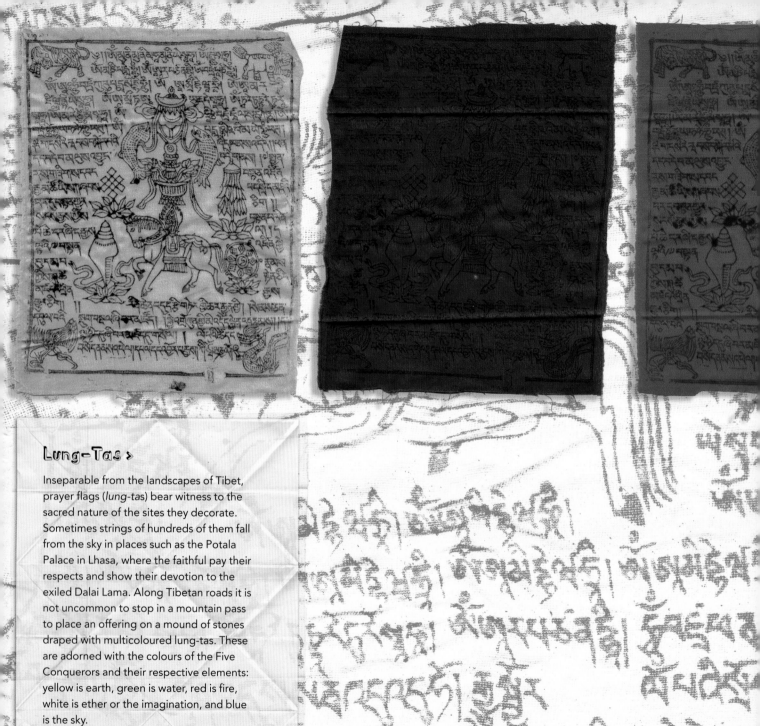

Lung-Tas ›

Inseparable from the landscapes of Tibet,
prayer flags (*lung-ta*s) bear witness to the
sacred nature of the sites they decorate.
Sometimes strings of hundreds of them fall
from the sky in places such as the Potala
Palace in Lhasa, where the faithful pay their
respects and show their devotion to the
exiled Dalai Lama. Along Tibetan roads it is
not uncommon to stop in a mountain pass
to place an offering on a mound of stones
draped with multicoloured lung-tas. These
are adorned with the colours of the Five
Conquerors and their respective elements:
yellow is earth, green is water, red is fire,
white is ether or the imagination, and blue
is the sky.

The concept of the lung-ta is said to have
been brought from India in the sixth century
by Atisha, an Indian Buddhist teacher who
was invited to Tibet by Yeshe Ö, ruler and
founder of the Guge Kingdom. Once in
Tibet, he taught how the sacred texts and

mantras of the many Buddhas could be printed on pieces of cloth. This soon became a popular custom since it was a progression of the ancient Bön religion, whose followers would hang pieces of wool on the trees as an offering and lucky charm.

It is thought that when a prayer flag is hung, the writings will be carried by the wind to touch every part of nature. It is considered an act of sharing and blessing, spreading Buddha's teachings throughout the world, and also an act of altruism, performed in the hope that all living things may be delivered from suffering.

Near prayer poles, yak horns engraved with the *Om Mani Padme Hum* mantra are often found to ward off evil spirits.

Darpoche >

Every year, on the first full
moon of April, the birth of
Buddha is commemorated.
Lamas and monks come
from far away for this
celebration and the
pilgrims join them to
receive their blessing.
It is customary to walk
around the flagpole while
the procession prepares
to raise it to the sound of
horns and tambourines.
The pole is soon lifted
up in a cloud of tsampa
(barley flour) and wind-
horses to the joyous cries
of the crowd.

The Way of Buddhism >

Mount Kailash and Manasarovar. Two sacred sites, two opposites; a masculine symbol and a feminine symbol. As eternal as the quest for Enlightenment, as eternal as birth and death. Unlike Christianity, Buddhism is free from dogma. 'The Passion of Christ happened once and is at the centre of the story of humanity. The birth and teachings of Buddha are repeated in cycles in every historical period.' (Jorge Luis Borges)

Like Christianity, it is based on the life of one figure, the historical Buddha Sakyamuni (sixth century BC), but Tibetan Buddhism is more willing to embrace spiritual concepts such as the mandala or the legend of the Five Conquerors, whose symbolism is easily understood; Mount Kailash itself is a good example of this.

For Hindus as well as Buddhists, life on Earth is a path towards perfection of the self.

The body, in conjunction with the mind, is the tool that creates a liberating force. As in Buddhism, the goal is to achieve complete detachment. The world is seen as a whole entity, and individuals may become one with the world around them when they feel a will to rid themselves of the poisons of existence (desire, hatred, ignorance) and escape from life's suffering.

PATCHOUPATH
NATH

28 October 1995. Gangri Chorten.

Two hours or so after passing the Gangri chorten, Thomas, who has stopped for a drink, points out to me a pack of half a dozen wild dogs. We stop to take a look at them. A few hundred metres away from us is a wave of beige and brown fur. The dogs are agitated. Our lives are worth little in the Kailash foothills.

Even in 1935, Giuseppe Tucci, the great Italian Tibetologist, described bandits descending from the hills to loot caravans, but that did not happen to us, thank God — and perhaps also thanks to the dogs who watched over the convoy. It makes us think about the journey ahead: those that we fear may also be those that save us. These dogs cannot be as vile as many Tibetans believe; the animals are regarded as low-level reincarnations and hence are often poorly treated.

28 October 1995. Nyanri Monastery.

The monk welcomes us with surprise and kindness, since few pilgrims make this detour. Once we have left our bags in the fuel shed that will be our bedroom, we follow our host to visit the building. In a prayer room, Thomas's face is suddenly lit up by the sun's rays let in by a small hole in the ceiling. With a mischievous smile, the monk shows us a little mirror hanging on the wall in which we can see the reflection of Kailash and its immaculate summit.

I am looking for a cheap/good hotel.
(අයි ඇම ලුකින් ෆො අ චීප්/ගුඩ හොටෙල්)
මම හොයන්නේ මිළ පහසු/හොඳ හෝටලයක්.
(mama hoyanne mila pahasu/honda hotalayak)

The View from Nyanri Monastery

Lake Manasarovar

Darpoche Pole

N

Gurla Mandata

Lake Rakastal

ll tornado

<-- Lhasa 900 km (550 miles) — Ali 300 km (180 miles) -->

South Valley. Ratnasambhava - Yellow Earth

Gangri Chorten

Pilgrim's Path

West Valley. Amitabha - Red Fire

Lingam: Shiva's Phallus

Yoni: Vagina

Cobra

29 October 1995. The Bull of Shiva.

A 1,000-metre rock face rises before me. This hiccup in the tectonic plate that touches the heavens is clearly a dream for any rock-climbing enthusiast, but the sport is completely forbidden on Mount Kailash, the home of the gods. For Hindus, this colossal rock represents Nandi, the bull of Shiva, an incarnation of the power attained through the control of passion, a quality granted to those that have achieved awareness. This 'vehicle' is the privilege of the strong, personifying uprightness and justice.

To the Hindus, Mount Kailash is Shiva's paradise, where he lives with his wife Parvati and their children, Ganesh and Skanda. The mountain and its alabaster summit are the lingam, Shiva's phallic emblem, symbolizing the energy of creation. The small steps seen on the southern slope represent the seven Lokas (degrees of perfection) that rise up to the god Shiva himself at the top.

Shiva and Parvati >

Shiva, the great god of destruction, he of a thousand names and a thousand tales. Like every figure in Hinduism, his character is complex. He must fight the forces of evil but is considered a god of creation. His third eye gives him wisdom while the other two, half-open, control the end of a cycle or the beginning of a new world with nothing more than a blink. With the gift of omniscient and transcendental vision that allows him to see the past (the energy of fire), the present (the sun) and the future (the moon), he may also become a ray of destruction when in a world of illusion. The sacred river, the Ganges, flows from his long hair, wrapped around his head and upon which sits a crescent-shaped moon, the symbol of the cycle of time. But the representation of Shiva that mostly closely fits Mount Kailash is that of Mahayogi, an ascetic symbolizing austerity, poverty and penance, seeking redemption in meditation.

‹ Sacred C

A sacred animal ev
ancient Mediterra
civilizations, the cow
been worshipped by Ind
since the Vedic pe
(1500–900 BC). For Hi
the cow is the symb
the earth, as it gives n
without asking anyt
in return. An obje
veneration and sacr
the cow and its product
pillars of Indian daily
milk, butter, meat fo
poor, its dung used as a
and a fertilizer and its
as a detergent. A sig
wealth and a piece of
equipment for peas
an aid to traffic contro
a means of waste disp
for city dwellers, ther
no less than twent
breeds of Indian
making up thirty per
of the world's lives

e American Staffordshire
rrier is a powerful dog
t first appeared at
 end of the nineteenth
ntury, introduced by
glish emigrants to the USA.
vas officially named in 1972.
eir strength and tenacious
ture were the result of
ng bred commercially
fighting dogs, originally
ainst pit bulls and other
 Staffs. Even today
ne breeders with little
nsideration for animal
ics raise such specimens,
own as game dogs.
e show dog has a cult
owing due to its strong
d supple physique. As a
mestic animal, the Am Staff
oved for its loyalty, agility
d good nature. Its cousin
 Staffordshire Bull Terrier is
en Britain's favourite dog!

18 September 1995. Benares.

In Benares the cremation ritual begins at the break of dawn, with the families bringing their loved ones' remains down to the river. The funeral pyres are set up on an esplanade above the ghats. Large piles of wood await in a small street down below; children climb up them to play. The smell of burning bodies is overwhelming. The smoke drifts off towards the horizon. Only the corpses of sadhus, children (who are considered pure), victims of snakebites and pregnant women have the right to be treated differently: wrapped in cloth and weighed down their bodies are given to the waters of the Ganges, the purifying river. In Tibet, apart from monks and lamas whose corpses are burnt, the funeral custom is to place the body of the deceased outside the village, preferably in a high location, where it is cut up and left for birds of prey. Buddhists prepare themselves for this end through meditation practice in which they visualize their own dismemberment.

I want a facial.
(අයි වොන්ට් අ ෆේෂල්)
මට ෆේෂල් එකක් කිරීමට අවශ්‍යයි.
(mata facial ekak kireemata avashyai)

What time does the show start.
(වට ටයිම් ඩස් ද ෂෝ ස්ටාට්)
දර්ශණය පටන් ගන්නේ කීයටද?
(dharshanaya patan ganne keeyatada?)

Sadhus ›

Many Westerners who visit Mount Kailash are bewildered by
the behaviour of the sadhus (sages). Travellers who have been to
India see the quest undertaken by these mystics as part of Hindu
folklore, but do not grasp the deeper truth behind their existence.

   The sadhu lives in a state of detachment from everything: from
himself and from worldly possessions. To achieve this he enters
the fourth stage of existence, that of total renunciation, the first
three stages being those of student and disciple, marriage and
professional activity, and retreat and relative poverty. The decision
to begin the fourth cycle, seen as being dead to this world, may be
taken at any time. The family will then prepare funeral rites for the
sadhu, delivering him from the chains of fate.

   The sadhu is the disciple of Shiva, and traditionally carries a
trident, symbol of the three *gunas*, or fundamental energies:
the energy of the mind (Shiva), of the soul (Vishnu) and of the body

›

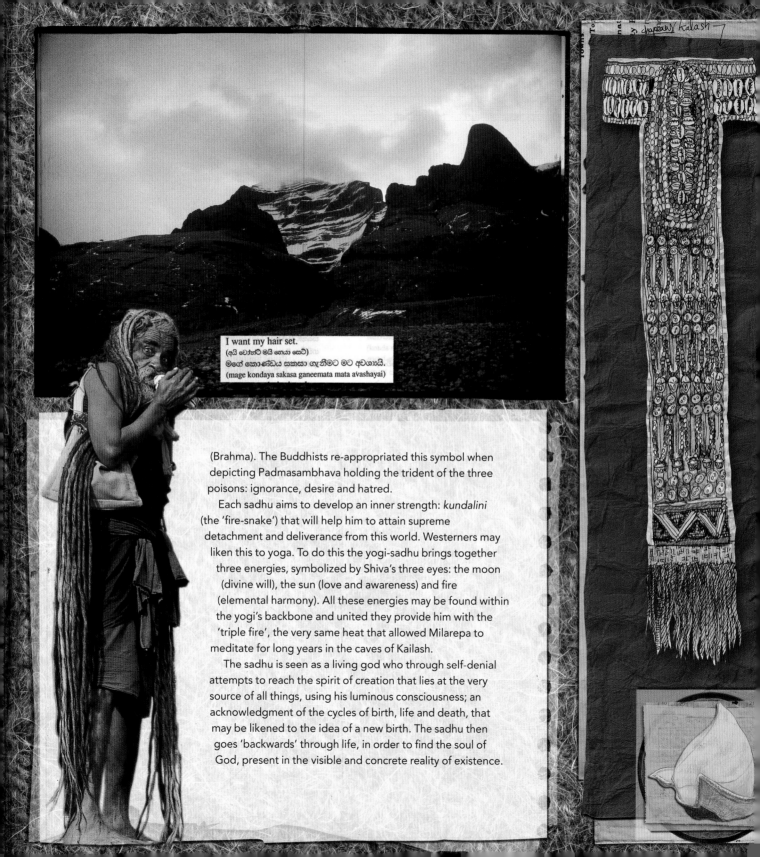

I want my hair set.
(අයි වෝන්ට් මයි හෙයා සෙට්)
මගේ කොණ්ඩය සකසා ගැනීමට මට අවශ්‍යයි.
(mage kondaya sakasa ganeemata mata avashayai)

(Brahma). The Buddhists re-appropriated this symbol when depicting Padmasambhava holding the trident of the three poisons: ignorance, desire and hatred.

Each sadhu aims to develop an inner strength: *kundalini* (the 'fire-snake') that will help him to attain supreme detachment and deliverance from this world. Westerners may liken this to yoga. To do this the yogi-sadhu brings together three energies, symbolized by Shiva's three eyes: the moon (divine will), the sun (love and awareness) and fire (elemental harmony). All these energies may be found within the yogi's backbone and united they provide him with the 'triple fire', the very same heat that allowed Milarepa to meditate for long years in the caves of Kailash.

The sadhu is seen as a living god who through self-denial attempts to reach the spirit of creation that lies at the very source of all things, using his luminous consciousness; an acknowledgment of the cycles of birth, life and death, that may be likened to the idea of a new birth. The sadhu then goes 'backwards' through life, in order to find the soul of God, present in the visible and concrete reality of existence.

28 December 1991. Kathmandu.

As soon as we finish the last mouthful of our breakfast, Thomas and I go out to discover Kathmandu. At the first street corner we come to, a gathering of the town folk, men women and children, catches our attention. A freshly killed buffalo lies on the ground, the sun's rays lighting up the trickles of blood spreading around the sacrificers' feet. Some men wielding simple knives cut the animal's head with difficulty. The spectacle is as fascinating as it is unpleasant, the smell of warm flesh overwhelming us. According to tradition, the body will be eaten by the crowd while the head is kept as an offering to the gods, placed in a small shrine with some incense. As soon as the bloody carcass is gone, the children begin to play in the thick pool, a sparkling myriad of crimson glints.

Sacrifice ›

By sacrificing a buffalo, Hindus destroy the vehicle used by Yama, the lord of death. The action is also a tribute to Durga, the Divine Mother (one of the manifestations of Parvati) who, in Hindu mythology, killed the demon Mahishasura while he was the form of a buffalo. Mahishasura had previously been granted invincibility by Brahma after years of penance.

29 October 1995. West Face.

At the back of a cold, drab and smelly room, Thomas and I mechanically make our beds for the night. A sleeping bag, my survival blanket, sweaters and anything dry and not too dirty for a pillow. Now is the moment to relish some of life's simple pleasures! First the socks! The effort needed to extract my sore heel from my clumpy shoe is as intense as the thrill that comes next, the refreshing encounter with air and water, the pure and the putrid, the hot and the cold. Next the delight of delights: to go inside the warmth of the soft cocoon-shaped bag.

But tonight I can't seem to get to sleep. I imagine myself lying on a *charpoy* (meaning 'four feet') in the heat of Benares. In the middle of the afternoon it is not uncommon to see Indians asleep in the middle of the street on these traditional beds made of wood and plaited rope. The very same ones are found in Pakistan or Nepal — the beds of course, not the Indians!

Gems ›

Beautiful and rare, jewels are seen by Westerners as decorative objects or symbols of status. In the Orient, however, they possess a language, a meaning, a power to absorb the energy of the cosmos.

The Indians, for whom astronomy is of great importance, use gems as talismans. In the days of the maharajas, their wives would regularly consult court astrologers to know which jewels to wear. While these ladies attended at sumptuous receptions and competed for the title of most beautiful, the planets above them continued to exert their influence on our earth. And so it was that for a pre-defined period, the women would be advised to wear agates, emeralds or aquamarines.

According to Hindu legend, the demon Vala was slain in battle and to spread his power, the gods transformed his body into a wealth of magnificent minerals: his blood became rubies, his eyes sapphires and his skin diamonds.

29 October 1995

17 November 1997

22 July 1994

29 October 1995. North Face.

This afternoon Thomas and I went for a long hike to the north face, following in the footsteps of Sven Hedin. In the early twentieth century this Swedish explorer was one of the first Westerners to witness this region's beauty. After three hours of exertion, we get close enough to gaze up at the 1,200 metres (4,000 feet) of rock face in front of us. The equivalent of four Eiffel Towers. Outrageous!

Thomas heads off towards the summit while I sketch this monument flanked by its two guards that represent the Buddhas Avalokitesvara (he who looks with eyes of compassion, the divinity of the Land of Snows) and Maitreya (he who pays homage, devoted to the master Sakyamuni).

In India there are many temples built in the image of Mount Kailash. The Kailashanatha is among the most famous. To reach its pyramidal tower, situated just behind the main building, several labyrinths must be crossed. Thomas must be wandering in a similar maze, up there on the glacier that I can hear cracking alarmingly. He reappears, shaken by this expedition to the heart of the moving mountain. Back home I would be moved myself when I realized that I had drawn the same panorama as Sven Hedin did, almost one hundred years ago.

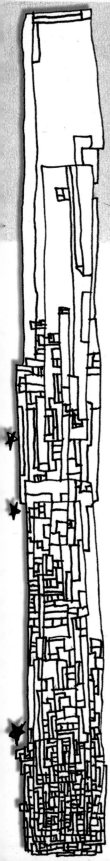

Taxila ›

Taxila, in the north of Pakistan, is today a city in ruins. But from the sixth century BC and for almost one thousand years, it was inhabited by a series of civilizations, making its ruins one of the most interesting archaeological sites of Gandhara art, a mixture of Greek and Indian cultures. Taxila may be split into several cities: Bhir Mound, Sirkap and Sirsukh.

Bhir Mound was described by the soldiers of Alexander the Great as a dirty and archaic town, whose inhabitants still practised human sacrifice, where the poorest sold their children and polygamy was allowed. It was not until the reign of the Indian King Ashoka that it became a busy cultural and trading centre. Ashoka, a great builder, established a single currency to facilitate trade and set up a university where the arts, mathematics, law, history, medicine and astronomy were taught. The remarkably well-run town, with its sewage system, rubbish bins and ramparts, was around one kilometre across. A symbol of tolerance, Bhir Mound was an important centre of religious exchange. Ashoka himself, after twelve years devoted to Shiva and to battles and conquests, converted to Buddhism and became a sworn pacifist. Many temples and religious monuments, such as the Dharmarajika Stupa, bear witness to his devotion.

In the second century BC, Sirkap was a far larger city, five kilometres across and stretching from the hills to the plain, its roads wide and its buildings impressive. It was inhabited by Greco-Bactrians. The town is described as being full of splendour

›

and wealth, with its businesses and great balconied houses, some of which possessed their own private stupas.

Sirsukh, a great fortress city situated to the north-east, was encircled by a thick wall. Excavations within the wall have not been possible because it surrounds a Muslim cemetery. The town was founded by the Kushans, originally from north China, who

reigned from the first to the third century AD over a region that stretched from the north of India to modern Afghanistan and Pakistan. Besides significant economic expansion, their

civilization was characterized by a widespread dissemination of writing and teaching, as well as considerable religious tolerance. In the city of Sirsukh, Zoroastrianism crossed paths with Hinduism, Buddhism and Greek pantheism.

In the middle of the fifth century AD, Taxila was destroyed by the Hephtalites, a Turkish-speaking nomadic tribe, barbarian and bloodthirsty.

Pen gun

26 March 2001. Afghanistan.

Kabul, August 2000: my brother Stéphane Allix, special correspondent and Afghanistan specialist, sets up the Afghan branch of the SDEF (Society of French Explorers). The first mission of this NGO (Non-Governmental Organization) is to draw up a catalogue of the country's cultural heritage, ravaged by twenty years of war and looting. Their first target: the Bamiyan valley and its great Buddhas sculpted in the rock.

Bamiyan ›

Bamiyan, city of caves and the marvellous heart of a trading civilization, located along the Silk Route. This is where the first human images of the Buddha Sakyamuni were made, in the first century AD. Four centuries earlier, Alexander the

Great, King of Macedonia, a great conqueror who died a the age of thirty-three, had pushed the limits of his empi to the banks of the Indus and laid the foundations of a ne civilization at the crossroads between China, the West a India. The Greeks, who had always depicted their gods in art, continued this tradition when some of them began t follow the teachings of Buddha. And so it was that the symbolic designs of wheels or lotuses were succeeded by faces sculpted in schist or stucco, inspired by Apollo, with masculine bodies, curly hair, almond eyes, long straight noses and full lips.

In the thirteenth century, Bamiyan was the scene of battles waged by the hordes of Genghis Khan, whose Mongol people adopted Tibetan Lamaism as their officia

...igion. But this was soon replaced by Islam and ...e conquest of Afghanistan by Timur Lang (...murlane) at the end of the fourteenth ...ntury, turning Kabul into the epicentre of ...ongol conquest.

...March 2001: The Taliban destroyed the ...useum of Kabul, in which were kept treasures ...covered by French archaeologist Alfred ...ucher during the last century. They also ...namited the Buddhas of Bamiyan, along with ...other non-Islamic divine representations. ...e scene of the disaster is visited by a convoy ...journalists. In the magnificent valley,

emotions run high. Not only have two 53- and 36-metre-high Buddhas been turned to dust, a little of every Afghan's heart has too. Never again will the faithful sit on the Buddha's heads to contemplate the view stretching before them with the strength of the Enlightened.

In the plane that takes us back to Kabul, I think back to the civilizations that once made Afghanistan a mecca for cultural exchange and knowledge, my sadness and melancholy only the beginning of an even greater pain.

12 April 2001. Ghazni, Afghanistan.

To bury someone is to bury a part of life, to bury memories, to bury a piece of oneself too. It is above all a need to face up to our own destiny, the mystery of the beyond that fills our souls with anguish. Death is the bombshell that lends a duality to life. Life and death, precious love and sickening fate, faith and ignorance, so many questions and so few answers.

Thomas was found on the road to Ghazni on 12 April 2001, the victim of a car accident, lying in the foetal position on the Afghan soil, his face peaceful and a slight smile on his lips. I had gone back to France a few hours earlier, my head still buzzing from the months spent in his company. Apart from the immense weight of grief that I must bear, I have learnt little by little to transform this pain into an elixir of life,

and to see his departure as the ultimate outcome of his Enlightenment. At the age of thirty my brother Thomas had assimilated the qualities of Buddhism: introspection through meditation, a respect for all beings and things, the importance of the beauty of the world and all its component parts, animal, vegetable, mineral and astral. On the day of his death he may have reached the peak of his incarnation, that of a sage that had lived on Kailash, the mountain that he adored and that he took me to discover.

It is now my turn to climb the steps of the mandala, and if the path is sometimes chaotic in our civilization where worries are often artificial, the charm of simple memories remains, like the hours spent together under a flowering apricot tree in the hills of Kabul, with the horizon as the sole witness to our supreme joy at being alive.

Vajrayogini Cemetery :

Just before arriving at the Dolma Pass, pilgrims leave some of their belongings at the cemetery dedicated to the female deity Vajrayogini. She is traditionally depicted naked but for a few characteristic items: necklace, *vajra*, earrings, bracelets and skirt. Her nakedness represents the freedom of her mind, free from the veils of ignorance and concepts forged by her mind. Her jewels represent the Six Perfections that must be attained: giving, ethics, patience, vigour, concentration and wisdom. All of these fundamental qualities may be passed on to pilgrims, who in return must make the gift of a possession, symbolizing their detachment from the world: hair, shoes, any sort of fabric or even a drop of blood. Sitting amongst the offerings

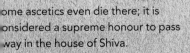

ome ascetics even die there; it is
onsidered a supreme honour to pass
way in the house of Shiva.

The Dolma Pass >

At 5,600 metres (over 18,000 feet) above sea level, the Dolma Pass (or Dolma-La) is the last point before the descent, the plain and Darchen; the last link to the heavens and the gods. The rocky chaos is criss-crossed with multicoloured ropes hung with lung-tas and pilgrims leaving their offerings. Their faces taut with exertion, they hang woollen yarn on to the rock or stick coins to it with a butter paste. Some even slip one of their teeth into its crannies.

Dolma is the Tibetan name for the Buddhist deity Tara ('she who saves'), a female bodhisattva who represents abandon: self-abandon, abandonment to faith, abandonment of suffering. Tara is a friendly deity, as her inspiration is that which is found at the root of all religions and her radiance that of a mother for her children. The arrival at the Dolma Pass rids the body of its burden of altitude and pain. Human beings are laid bare before Tara, the goddess of compassion, who will help them to be born again. She also represents the *prajnaparamita*, the ability to discover the reality or unreality of things, which is the beginning of Enlightenment.

30 October 1995. Dolma-La.

The last few metres before arriving at the great Dolma-La boulder are very tiring. My brother had told me stories from his previous pilgrimages, his impressions of being purged when approaching the summit. The moment when there is no more effort, when your whole body carries you towards the beyond, to the other side of the rock, where a second life begins that is free of all demands.

I do not think, I am only movement, an animal climbing up, jolting through the crowds of Tibetans murmuring 'Sososososo', their incantation of thanks to the gods that seems to hypnotize them during this final burst of effort. Traditionally the arrival at the Dolma-La is accompanied by a flash of consciousness, like a logical reply to the power of White Tara, the maternal and protective deity whose mission is to come to our aid.

Guri Kund >

The Lake of Compassion

30 October 1995. The music of silence.
My eyes drift off into the green and grey expanse of rocks. An unknown landscape that seems familiar, a lightness of limbs and a violent yearning for sensations. I raise my arms to melt into the deep blue of the sky, the insatiable hunger of a mind drifting into infinity. My body rocks and jolts, this movement my very own music. I walk like an improvising soloist, free but full of zeal. Each note rings with an informed sensitivity, like that of the great musicians who have understood the importance of silence and whose subtle efforts strive to make the mirror of our emotions shine.

28 August 1994. Benares.

Between flight and contemplation, the journey is full of
the expectation of sensations whose purest form is always
that of a gaze full of complicity and serenity.

Is it because every dazzling sight seems to make
time stand still for the traveller? Here gestures have a
sensuality that seems to be rooted in tradition. Move by
move, the actors in this great theatre, this town where
life never stops, play their parts in the chaos of merging
crowds, traffic, noise and smells. Their wisdom arouses
respect and plunges the traveller into the divine motor
of Benares, its spirituality.

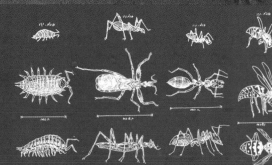

The Bhopal Disaster >

India is a land of contrasts. From the most beautiful to the ugliest, the most elegant to the dirtiest, every moment shared with this country vibrates with a thousand emotions. The magnetism of its imagery is so great that a mere glimpse can touch the right chord and change you forever. When witnessing the poverty in which part of the population lives, stepping over corpses in the street, one's feelings vacillate between compassion and disgust; this is particularly so when such horror is the result of dangerous industries installed right at the heart of these communities. This was the case of the Bhopal catastrophe which even today continues to poison the water wells of over 200,000 people.

In December 1984, a gas leak at the Union Carbide factory (a pesticide manufacturer) killed 30,000 people in Bhopal. Four years later the industrial site was abandoned. Its director, still in hiding, is wanted by Interpol. Since then, chemical waste has infiltrated the ground water, resulting in hormonal problems (the menopause at age 25), cancers and deformities. The files concerning the sanitary analyses have disappeared from the Indian officials' offices. Despite cries of alarm from many NGOs, this disaster was given significantly less media coverage than that of Chernobyl which took place a year later and killed fewer people.

Because Union Carbide kept its manufacturing processes secret, no efficient medical treatment could be developed. Some 20 per cent of the population has access to the drinking water trucks chartered by the local council, but the trucks must reach them first. Thousands of victims are given aid by private projects, such as the Dominique Lapierre Clinic.

30 October 1995. The Descent.

The exhilaration of the descent becomes ethereal, my physical strain a thing of the past. I float in an ocean of colours and light. Nature has never seemed so radiant, each detail encapsulating a dazzling vision of a world in which the rocks and plants form a divine palette of colours, all shining with a unique radiance.

I feel like the first man to tread this earth, filled with calm. The last stage of the pilgrimage corresponds to the fourth petal of the lotus, the sign of water. The universal element of purity and life raises me up, and I am overwhelmed by a feeling of lightness, a sense of renewal. For the first time the communion with nature heightens my senses; more than just seeing its majesty, I feel its living strength.

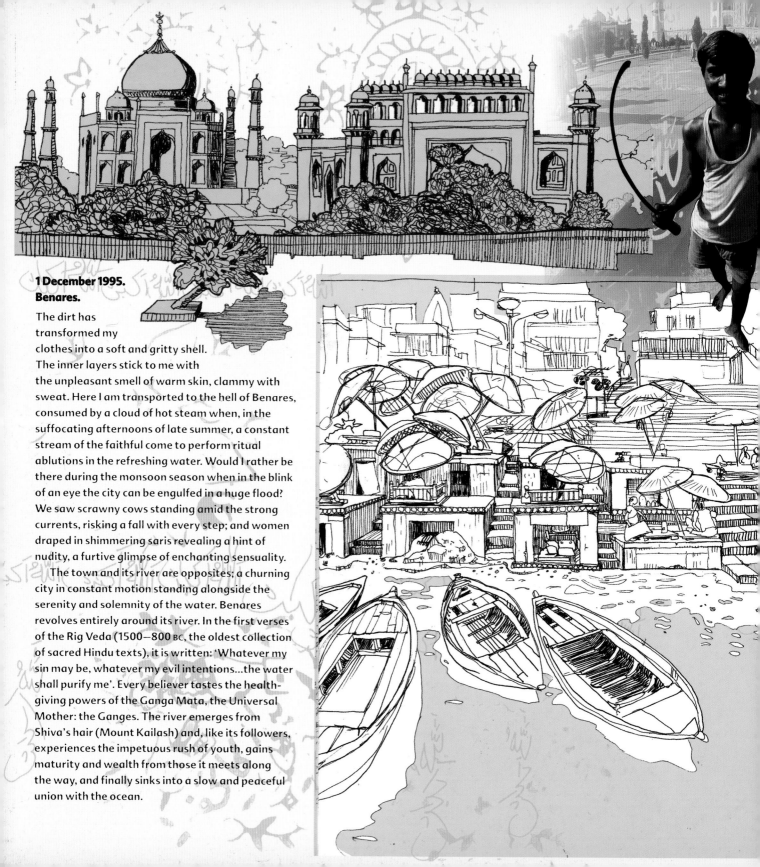

1 December 1995.
Benares.

The dirt has transformed my clothes into a soft and gritty shell. The inner layers stick to me with the unpleasant smell of warm skin, clammy with sweat. Here I am transported to the hell of Benares, consumed by a cloud of hot steam when, in the suffocating afternoons of late summer, a constant stream of the faithful come to perform ritual ablutions in the refreshing water. Would I rather be there during the monsoon season when in the blink of an eye the city can be engulfed in a huge flood? We saw scrawny cows standing amid the strong currents, risking a fall with every step; and women draped in shimmering saris revealing a hint of nudity, a furtive glimpse of enchanting sensuality.

The town and its river are opposites; a churning city in constant motion standing alongside the serenity and solemnity of the water. Benares revolves entirely around its river. In the first verses of the Rig Veda (1500–800 BC, the oldest collection of sacred Hindu texts), it is written: 'Whatever my sin may be, whatever my evil intentions...the water shall purify me'. Every believer tastes the health-giving powers of the Ganga Mata, the Universal Mother: the Ganges. The river emerges from Shiva's hair (Mount Kailash) and, like its followers, experiences the impetuous rush of youth, gains maturity and wealth from those it meets along the way, and finally sinks into a slow and peaceful union with the ocean.

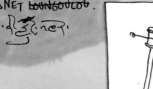
LOU-NGOR
MANET ~~LOUNGOULOU~~.
অইচ্রূন্থর।

MANET LACO'R
অইন্ম্যান্র্থী।

sur les toit.
THOU
অহুৰী।

LOUGDA
হ্রীক্রি

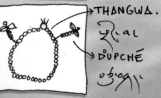
→THANGWA.
হ্রীঅল
→DUPCHÉ
ওর্ঞেঞ্জী

DORDGÉ
ক্রন্ত্রী
→thilou.
ষ্ট্রন্মীঘ্যি

GARDZEN
হ্রন্মব্র্ষী

DAR-C
Kiak

Milarepa >

The region around Mount Kailash echoes with the songs and miracles of the monk and poet Milarepa (1040–1125). He is the focus of a major cult, having practised meditation and asceticism for many years while writing poems glorifying the Buddha and his teachings. But in popular imagery, Milarepa is perhaps best known as the vanquisher of the Bön wizard, Naro Bonchung, whom he challenged at the foot of the sacred mountain.

Milarepa's life is highly complex and full of miraculous encounters and symbolism. Like many divinities and other real-life figures that became sacred (such as Padmasambhava), his life contained suffering and revenge as well as devotion, meditation and finally Enlightenment.

From his first lessons from a master of black magic that helped him to avenge his family, who had been left destitute by unscrupulous relatives, to his redemption by his guru Marpa (a disciple of Naropa, the incarnation of Avalokitesvara) who taught him the art of meditation, Milarepa's life speaks of the importance of karma, of actions and their consequences. He was aided by the mental and physical powers that he was endowed with, his perfect command of Tum-Mo (in which the person meditating produces enough energy to resist the cold) and above all his wish to go far away from the rest of mankind in order to look inside himself and discover the true nature of mind.

When he arrived at Mount Kailash, where his master had encouraged him to go to meditate, Milarepa already had an idea of the life that awaited him, that of an ascetic seeking the supreme state, that of *bodhisattva*, of Enlightenment. He began his work in a cave, and when his provisions had run out, he fed himself on the weeds that grew nearby. His body grew thin and little by little his hair began to turn green as he went deeper and deeper into his meditation.

One day a Bön magician, Naro Bonchung, appeared and they quarrelled about who had the right to the sacred mountain. The magician argued that Mount Kailash had traditionally belonged to his people for thousands of years, but Milarepa replied that the powers of the Buddha were greater. So, to settle the argument, they each put their own powers to the test. Milarepa lay on Lake Manasarovar while singing an ode to the glory of the Buddha's teachings. Then he pointed to some rocks and they formed a pile on their own, creating a cave known as the Cave of Miracles, in which Milarepa lived from that day on. According to the legend, Milarepa left his handprints on the cave's ceiling and his footprints on its roof, and made it bigger or smaller according to the season.

The Bön magician was unable to defeat such powers, but he would not give up. He suggested one final test: he who climbed the mountain the fastest the following morning would dethrone the other's religion. At the crack of dawn the magician flew into the air with his magic drum. Milarepa watched him rise from the bottom of the mountain when all of a sudden the first rays of sun appeared. Becoming one with the light, he arrived at the top before the magician. Surprised to see his rival at the summit, the magician dropped his drum which fell tumbling down, creating the great gash that can still be seen cutting through the rocky strata of the southern slope. This feat symbolized the supremacy of Buddhism over the ancient Bön faith.

Milarepa soon began to shine with spiritual light, spreading Enlightenment all around and banishing ignorance and egotism.

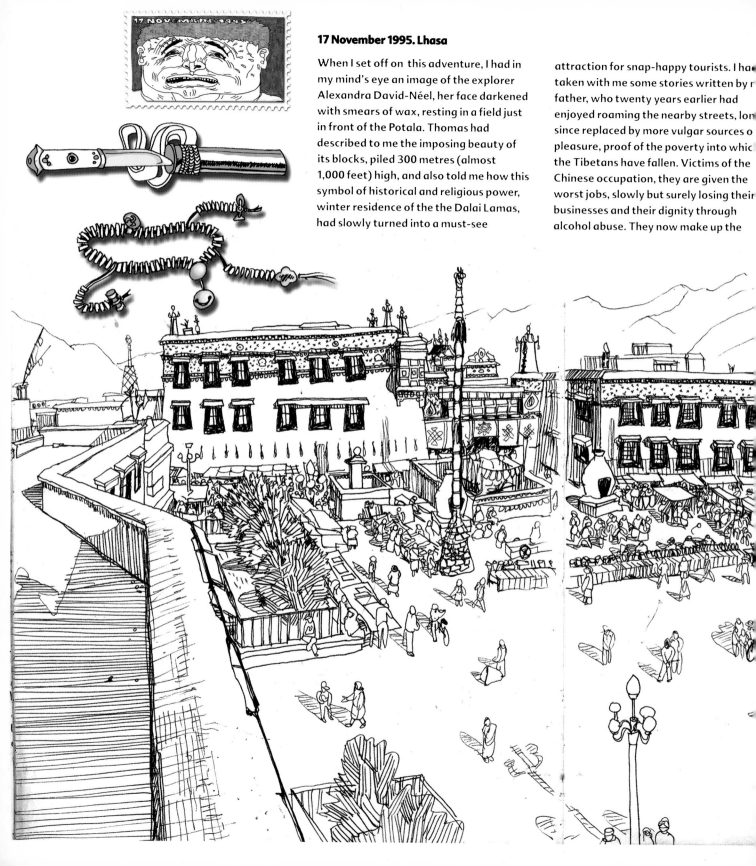

17 November 1995. Lhasa

When I set off on this adventure, I had in my mind's eye an image of the explorer Alexandra David-Néel, her face darkened with smears of wax, resting in a field just in front of the Potala. Thomas had described to me the imposing beauty of its blocks, piled 300 metres (almost 1,000 feet) high, and also told me how this symbol of historical and religious power, winter residence of the the Dalai Lamas, had slowly turned into a must-see attraction for snap-happy tourists. I ha[d] taken with me some stories written by [my] father, who twenty years earlier had enjoyed roaming the nearby streets, lon[g] since replaced by more vulgar sources o[f] pleasure, proof of the poverty into whic[h] the Tibetans have fallen. Victims of the Chinese occupation, they are given the worst jobs, slowly but surely losing their businesses and their dignity through alcohol abuse. They now make up the crowds of prostitutes and beggars that wander the huge squares lit by lofty lamps, at the foot of monuments to their former splendour, testimony to a bygone golden age.

LA VICTIME

PINE-ZOB, PILOTE DE BUS CHINOIS — PORTRAIT ROBOT

① SIMOB DIT LE FOU
② PHIPHI L'ÉTRANGLEUR
③ VINCENT LA TORTURE
④ MAO LOUMPO
⑤ THOMAS LONG COUTEAU

LES ASSASSINS PRÉSUMÉS

LE DORDGÉ

LES ARMES DU CRIME

LE THERMOS

LE DUVET IMPERMÉABLE

LE CRIC

LE MOULIN A PRIÈRE

LE COUTELAS

LE STYLO PERDU

L'APPAREIL PHOTO

LES LIEUX DU CRIME

LES AUTRES ARMES

LA CABINE DU CHAUFEUR

LES CHIOTTES DU YAK HOTEL

LAC MANASAROVAR

LA CHAMBRE A 50 YUANS

LE PUITS DE TINGRI

PORTRAIT DE MAO

BOUTEILLE DE BIÈRE

LE JERRICAN D'ESSENCE

LA PSB D'ALI

LA MOTO DE SAN-KOUKSY

L'ASSIETTE DE MOMOS

LE CHAPELET

LA BOÎTE DE COCHON CHINOIS

mais qui a tué pine-zob?

RÉPONSE: MAO-LOUMPO LE COLABO

The Potala ≻

Like the Jokhang Temp[le]
the Potala was originall[y]
built by Songtsen Gam[po]
the great reformer who
introduced the idea of
dynastic power to Tibe[t]
in the seventh century,
uniting the influential
families under his
sovereignty. It was also
during his reign that
Buddhism came to Tibe[t]
so he was therefore
held in great religious
esteem. The building w[as]
damaged in several wa[ys]
and had to wait for the
second half of the
seventeenth century an[d]
the arrival of the Fifth D[alai]
Lama, Ngawang Lobsa[ng]
Gyatso, before becomi[ng]
the finished constructio[n]
that can be admired tod[ay].
The palace named afte[r]
Mount Potala, a sacred
mountain in the south o[f]
India, which is linked to
Shiva by the Hindus and
to Avalokitesvara by
Buddhists. Songtsen
Gampo and the Dalai
Lamas were considered
reincarnations of
Avalokitesvara, a kindly
divinity and the protect[or]
of Tibet; this explains h[ow]
the Potala, although un[der]
siege by Chinese ceme[nt],
has survived revolution[s]
and conflicts, watched
over by this god.

Epilogue ›

It has been a long time since I left the foothills of Mount Kailash, the pilgrims and their mantras, the light full of life and the fantastic colours that make this region the jewel of ancient religions. Although from the foot of the mountain, the journey can be tough and the effort required is as powerful as the place itself, the memories remain, secretly pigmenting my own mandala and adding spice to my daily life. The stunning perfection of Kailash is beyond compare, and it would be futile to seek its secret, other than considering its majesty as absolute, a source of sustenance along the road to Enlightenment.

'The spiritual quest is an ascension, the paths leading to the summit are many and of diverse lengths, and necessarily so, as men think, understand and feel differently. While the paths may be different, the goal is unique.'

(Bhumananda, Indian ascetic and spiritual guide to Giuseppe Tucci during his expedition to Mount Kailash in 1935.)

Further Reading

Recommended:

Kailas: On Pilgrimage to the Sacred Mountain of Tibet
Russell Johnson and Kerry Moran, London 1990
A wonderful book with lively and sensitive texts, full of historical and
ethnological information on the pilgrimage and the mountain.
A passionate work of reference, illustrated with magnificent photos.

The Tibet Guide
Stephen Batchelor, London, 1987
400 very well-documented pages guiding the traveller through all
aspects of Tibet and its history. A treasure trove.

Tibet: Land of Snows
Giuseppe Tucci, London, 1967
A book by the Italian professor Giuseppe Tucci, presenting the
history, religion, art and daily life of Tibet. The scholarship and
straightforwardness of this great specialist make his writings
fascinating testimonies of a past age and of his spirit of adventure,
his thirst for knowledge and his lucidity.

Kailash, montagne sacrée du Tibet
Michel Coquet, Paris, 1989
A captivating little book analysing the mystical aspects of
Mount Kailash and its religious symbols. An excellent work
of synthesis and an inspiring read.

Buddhist Himalayas: People, Faith and Nature
Matthieu Ricard and Danielle and Olivier Föllmi, London, 2002
An unprecedented visual testimony compiling the most beautiful
photographs taken by the Föllmis and Matthieu Ricard, one of the
major French Buddhist scholars.

Other Titles of Interest:

The Wisdom of the Buddha,
Jean Boisselier, New York, 1994

Qué es el Budismo,
Jorge Luis Borges with Alicia Jurado, Barcelona, 1991

Tibet: Turning the Wheel of Life,
Françoise Pommaret,
London, 2003

The Monk and the Philosopher,
Jean François Revel
and Matthieu Ricard, New York, 1999

*Petite encyclopédie des divinités et symboles
du bouddhisme tibétain*,
Tcheuky Sèngué, Saint-Cannat, 2002

The Paths of Buddhism,
Jean-Luc Toula-Breysse, London, 2001

Crazy Wisdom,
Chögyam Trungpa, Boston, 1991

*The Himalaya–Kailasa–Manasarovar
in Scripture, Art and Thought*,
Rommel and Sadhana Varma, Geneva, 1985

Picture Credits

Drawings, paintings, maps, photomontages
© *Simon Allix*

Photographs © *Simon Allix and Thomas Allix*
with the exception of the following:

pp. 28–29. Waterfall © *Jean-Pierre Allix*

pp. 38–39. Relief plan © *Jean-Pierre Allix*

pp. 48–49. Thomas © *Ronit Pardo*

p. 60. Poster © *K. P. Seveul*

p. 61. Am Staff © *Anthony Daquila*

pp. 82–83. © *Simon Allix* for
Mandarava Productions 2001

pp. 84–85. Thomas in Jordan © *Ronit Pardo*

pp. 86–87. Motorcyclist © *Vadim Schoeffel*

pp. 110–111. Thomas © *Vincent Pignon*

pp. 36–37, 40, 74–75, 86, 104. Illustrations
of Buddhist deities from *Petite encyclopédie
des divinités et symboles du bouddhisme
tibétain* by Tcheuky Sèngué, published by
Editions Claire Lumière, 5 av. Camille Pelletan,
13760 Saint-Cannat, France. Reproduced with
the author's permission.

Acknowledgments

Jean-Pierre Allix
Claude Allix
Stéphane Allix
Tifenn A.
La Guilde Européenne du Raid
Claude Collin Delavaud
Priscilla Telmon
Tarak Maklouf
Anthony Daquila USK
Ronit Pardo
Etienne Sevet
Eve Prangey
Flore Masure
Popay
Céline Pré
Fred Cipola & Nino
Sylvain Tesson
Snafu
Patrice Franseschi
Le Riscquat
Pascale Lemoine
Francine Tissot
Arnaud Gouallec
Vincent & Philippe
F. Schubert & Dr L. Subramaniam
Thames & Hudson

*and all our friends
who have supported this project!*